Begin each day with a grateful heart.

Date:___/___/___
S / M / T / W / T / F / S

Inspirational Quote:

_____

_____

Morning Intentions

Daily Affirmation:

_____

_____

Today, I look forward to...

_____

_____

What would make today amazing?

_____

_____

Evening Reflections

What would make today greater?

_____

_____

Best Moment of My Day:

_____

_____

People I am grateful for...

_____

REMEMBER:

_____

Tomorrow I am looking forward to...

_____

_____

Journal Prompt

FREE YOURSELF !

Inspirational Quote:

Date: ___/___/___
S / M / T / W / T / F / S

Morning Intentions

Daily Affirmation:

Today, I look forward to…

What would make today amazing?

Evening Reflections

What would make today greater?

Best Moment of My Day:

People I am grateful for…

REMEMBER:

Tomorrow I am looking forward to…

Journal Prompt
FREE YOURSELF !

Inspirational Quote:

Date:___/___/___
S / M / T / W / T / F / S

Morning Intentions

Daily Affirmation:

Today, I look forward to...

What would make today amazing?

Evening Reflections

What would make today greater?

Best Moment of My Day:

People I am grateful for...

REMEMBER:

Tomorrow I am looking forward to...

Journal Prompt
FREE YOURSELF !

Date:___/___/___
S / M / T / W / T / F / S

Inspirational Quote:

Morning Intentions

Daily Affirmation:

Today, I look forward to...

What would make today amazing?

Evening Reflections

What would make today greater?

Best Moment of My Day:

People I am grateful for...

REMEMBER:

Tomorrow I am looking forward to...

Journal Prompt

FREE YOURSELF !

Inspirational Quote:

Date:___/___/___
S / M / T / W / T / F / S

Morning Intentions

Daily Affirmation:

Today, I look forward to...

What would make today amazing?

Evening Reflections

What would make today greater?

Best Moment of My Day:

People I am grateful for...

REMEMBER:

Tomorrow I am looking forward to...

Journal Prompt
FREE YOURSELF !

Inspirational Quote:

Date: ___/___/___
S / M / T / W / T / F / S

Morning Intentions

Daily Affirmation:

Today, I look forward to...

What would make today amazing?

Evening Reflections

What would make today greater?

Best Moment of My Day:

People I am grateful for...

REMEMBER:

Tomorrow I am looking forward to...

Journal Prompt

FREE YOURSELF !

Date:___/___/___
S / M / T / W / T / F / S

Inspirational Quote:

Morning Intentions

Daily Affirmation:

Today, I look forward to...

What would make today amazing?

Evening Reflections

What would make today greater?

Best Moment of My Day:

People I am grateful for...

REMEMBER:

Tomorrow I am looking forward to...

Journal Prompt

FREE YOURSELF !

Date: ___/___/___
S / M / T / W / T / F / S

Inspirational Quote:

Morning Intentions

Daily Affirmation:

Today, I look forward to...

What would make today amazing?

Evening Reflections

What would make today greater?

Best Moment of My Day:

People I am grateful for...

REMEMBER:

Tomorrow I am looking forward to...

Journal Prompt

FREE YOURSELF !

Inspirational Quote:

Date:___/___/___
S / M / T / W / T / F / S

Morning Intentions

Daily Affirmation:

Today, I look forward to...

What would make today amazing?

Evening Reflections

What would make today greater?

Best Moment of My Day:

People I am grateful for...

REMEMBER:

Tomorrow I am looking forward to...

Journal Prompt

FREE YOURSELF !

Date: ___/___/___
S / M / T / W / T / F / S

Inspirational Quote:

Morning Intentions

Daily Affirmation:

Today, I look forward to...

What would make today amazing?

Evening Reflections

What would make today greater?

Best Moment of My Day:

People I am grateful for...

REMEMBER:

Tomorrow I am looking forward to...

Journal Prompt

FREE YOURSELF !

Date: ___/___/___
S / M / T / W / T / F / S

Inspirational Quote:

Morning Intentions

Daily Affirmation:

Today, I look forward to...

What would make today amazing?

Evening Reflections

What would make today greater?

Best Moment of My Day:

People I am grateful for...

REMEMBER:

Tomorrow I am looking forward to...

Journal Prompt

FREE YOURSELF !

Date: ___/___/___
S / M / T / W / T / F / S

Inspirational Quote:

Morning Intentions

Daily Affirmation:

Today, I look forward to...

What would make today amazing?

Evening Reflections

What would make today greater?

Best Moment of My Day:

People I am grateful for...

REMEMBER:

Tomorrow I am looking forward to...

Journal Prompt

FREE YOURSELF !

Date: ___/___/___
S / M / T / W / T / F / S

Inspirational Quote:
_____
_____

Morning Intentions

Daily Affirmation:
_____
_____
_____

Today, I look forward to...
_____
_____
_____

What would make today amazing?
_____
_____
_____

Evening Reflections

What would make today greater?
_____
_____
_____

Best Moment of My Day:
_____
_____
_____

People I am grateful for...
_____
_____
_____

REMEMBER:

Tomorrow I am looking forward to...
_____
_____

Journal Prompt

FREE YOURSELF !

Inspirational Quote:

Date: ___/___/___
S / M / T / W / T / F / S

___

Morning Intentions

Daily Affirmation:
___
___
___

Today, I look forward to...
___
___
___

What would make today amazing?
___
___
___

Evening Reflections

What would make today greater?
___
___
___

Best Moment of My Day:
___
___
___

People I am grateful for...
___
___

REMEMBER:

Tomorrow I am looking forward to...
___
___

Journal Prompt

FREE YOURSELF !

Inspirational Quote:

Date:___/___/___
S / M / T / W / T / F / S

Morning Intentions

Daily Affirmation:

Today, I look forward to...

What would make today amazing?

Evening Reflections

What would make today greater?

Best Moment of My Day:

People I am grateful for...

REMEMBER:

Tomorrow I am looking forward to...

Journal Prompt

FREE YOURSELF !

Inspirational Quote:

Date: ___/___/___
S / M / T / W / T / F / S

Morning Intentions

Daily Affirmation:

Today, I look forward to...

What would make today amazing?

Evening Reflections

What would make today greater?

Best Moment of My Day:

People I am grateful for...

REMEMBER:

Tomorrow I am looking forward to...

Journal Prompt

FREE YOURSELF !

Date:___/___/___
S / M / T / W / T / F / S

Inspirational Quote:

Morning Intentions

Daily Affirmation:

Today, I look forward to...

What would make today amazing?

Evening Reflections

What would make today greater?

Best Moment of My Day:

People I am grateful for...

REMEMBER:

Tomorrow I am looking forward to...

Journal Prompt

FREE YOURSELF !

Date:___/___/___
S / M / T / W / T / F / S

Inspirational Quote:

Morning Intentions

Daily Affirmation:

Today, I look forward to...

What would make today amazing?

Evening Reflections

What would make today greater?

Best Moment of My Day:

People I am grateful for...

REMEMBER:

Tomorrow I am looking forward to...

Journal Prompt

FREE YOURSELF !

Date:___/___/___
S / M / T / W / T / F / S

Inspirational Quote:

Morning Intentions

Daily Affirmation:

Today, I look forward to...

What would make today amazing?

Evening Reflections

What would make today greater?

Best Moment of My Day:

People I am grateful for...

REMEMBER:

Tomorrow I am looking forward to...

Journal Prompt

FREE YOURSELF !

Inspirational Quote:

Date:___/___/___
S / M / T / W / T / F / S

Morning Intentions

Daily Affirmation:

Today, I look forward to...

What would make today amazing?

Evening Reflections

What would make today greater?

Best Moment of My Day:

People I am grateful for...

REMEMBER:

Tomorrow I am looking forward to...

Journal Prompt

FREE YOURSELF !

Inspirational Quote:

Date:___/___/___
S / M / T / W / T / F / S

Morning Intentions

Daily Affirmation:

Today, I look forward to...

What would make today amazing?

Evening Reflections

What would make today greater?

Best Moment of My Day:

People I am grateful for...

REMEMBER:

Tomorrow I am looking forward to...

Journal Prompt

FREE YOURSELF !

Date: ___/___/___
S / M / T / W / T / F / S

Inspirational Quote:

___

Morning Intentions

Daily Affirmation:

___

Today, I look forward to...

___

What would make today amazing?

___

Evening Reflections

What would make today greater?

___

Best Moment of My Day:

___

People I am grateful for...

REMEMBER:

Tomorrow I am looking forward to...

___

Journal Prompt

FREE YOURSELF !

Inspirational Quote:

Date: ___/___/___
S / M / T / W / T / F / S

Morning Intentions

Daily Affirmation:

Today, I look forward to...

What would make today amazing?

Evening Reflections

What would make today greater?

Best Moment of My Day:

People I am grateful for...

REMEMBER:

Tomorrow I am looking forward to...

Journal Prompt

FREE YOURSELF !

Date:___/___/___
S / M / T / W / T / F / S

Inspirational Quote:

Morning Intentions

Daily Affirmation:

Today, I look forward to...

What would make today amazing?

Evening Reflections

What would make today greater?

Best Moment of My Day:

People I am grateful for...

REMEMBER:

Tomorrow I am looking forward to...

Journal Prompt
FREE YOURSELF !

Inspirational Quote:

Date:___/___/___
S / M / T / W / T / F / S

Morning Intentions

Daily Affirmation:

Today, I look forward to...

What would make today amazing?

Evening Reflections

What would make today greater?

Best Moment of My Day:

People I am grateful for...

REMEMBER:

Tomorrow I am looking forward to...

Journal Prompt

FREE YOURSELF !

Inspirational Quote:

Date:___/___/___
S / M / T / W / T / F / S

_____
_____

Morning Intentions

Daily Affirmation:
_____
_____

Today, I look forward to...
_____
_____

What would make today amazing?
_____
_____

Evening Reflections

What would make today greater?
_____
_____

Best Moment of My Day:
_____
_____

People I am grateful for...
_____

REMEMBER:

_____

Tomorrow I am looking forward to...
_____
_____

Journal Prompt
FREE YOURSELF !

Inspirational Quote:

Date:___/___/___
S / M / T / W / T / F / S

Morning Intentions

Daily Affirmation:

Today, I look forward to...

What would make today amazing?

Evening Reflections

What would make today greater?

Best Moment of My Day:

People I am grateful for...

REMEMBER:

Tomorrow I am looking forward to...

Journal Prompt

FREE YOURSELF !

Inspirational Quote:

Date:___/___/___
S / M / T / W / T / F / S

Morning Intentions

Daily Affirmation:

Today, I look forward to...

What would make today amazing?

Evening Reflections

What would make today greater?

Best Moment of My Day:

People I am grateful for...

REMEMBER:

Tomorrow I am looking forward to...

Journal Prompt

FREE YOURSELF !

Inspirational Quote:

Date:___/___/___
S / M / T / W / T / F / S

Morning Intentions

Daily Affirmation:

Today, I look forward to...

What would make today amazing?

Evening Reflections

What would make today greater?

Best Moment of My Day:

People I am grateful for...

REMEMBER:

Tomorrow I am looking forward to...

Journal Prompt

FREE YOURSELF !

Date:___/___/___
S / M / T / W / T / F / S

Inspirational Quote:

Morning Intentions

Daily Affirmation:

Today, I look forward to...

What would make today amazing?

Evening Reflections

What would make today greater?

Best Moment of My Day:

People I am grateful for...

REMEMBER:

Tomorrow I am looking forward to...

Journal Prompt

FREE YOURSELF !

Date:___/___/___
S / M / T / W / T / F / S

Inspirational Quote:

Morning Intentions

Daily Affirmation:

Today, I look forward to...

What would make today amazing?

Evening Reflections

What would make today greater?

Best Moment of My Day:

People I am grateful for...

REMEMBER:

Tomorrow I am looking forward to...

Journal Prompt

FREE YOURSELF !

Inspirational Quote:

Date:___/___/___
S / M / T / W / T / F / S

Morning Intentions

Daily Affirmation:

Today, I look forward to...

What would make today amazing?

Evening Reflections

What would make today greater?

Best Moment of My Day:

People I am grateful for...

REMEMBER:

Tomorrow I am looking forward to...

Journal Prompt

FREE YOURSELF !

Inspirational Quote:

Date:___/___/___
S / M / T / W / T / F / S

Morning Intentions

Daily Affirmation:

Today, I look forward to...

What would make today amazing?

Evening Reflections

What would make today greater?

Best Moment of My Day:

People I am grateful for...

REMEMBER:

Tomorrow I am looking forward to...

Journal Prompt

FREE YOURSELF !

Inspirational Quote:

Date:___/___/___
S / M / T / W / T / F / S

Morning Intentions

Daily Affirmation:

Today, I look forward to...

What would make today amazing?

Evening Reflections

What would make today greater?

Best Moment of My Day:

People I am grateful for...

REMEMBER:

Tomorrow I am looking forward to...

Journal Prompt

FREE YOURSELF !

Date: ___/___/___
S / M / T / W / T / F / S

Inspirational Quote:

Morning Intentions

Daily Affirmation:

Today, I look forward to...

What would make today amazing?

Evening Reflections

What would make today greater?

Best Moment of My Day:

People I am grateful for...

REMEMBER:

Tomorrow I am looking forward to...

Journal Prompt

FREE YOURSELF !

Inspirational Quote:

Date:___/___/___
S / M / T / W / T / F / S

Morning Intentions

Daily Affirmation:

Today, I look forward to...

What would make today amazing?

Evening Reflections

What would make today greater?

Best Moment of My Day:

People I am grateful for...

REMEMBER:

Tomorrow I am looking forward to...

Journal Prompt

FREE YOURSELF !

Date:___/___/___
S / M / T / W / T / F / S

Inspirational Quote:

Morning Intentions

Daily Affirmation:

Today, I look forward to...

What would make today amazing?

Evening Reflections

What would make today greater?

Best Moment of My Day:

People I am grateful for...

REMEMBER:

Tomorrow I am looking forward to...

Journal Prompt

FREE YOURSELF !

Inspirational Quote:

Date:___/___/___
S / M / T / W / T / F / S

Morning Intentions

Daily Affirmation:

Today, I look forward to...

What would make today amazing?

Evening Reflections

What would make today greater?

Best Moment of My Day:

People I am grateful for...

REMEMBER:

Tomorrow I am looking forward to...

Journal Prompt

FREE YOURSELF !

Date:___/___/___
S / M / T / W / T / F / S

Inspirational Quote:
_____
_____

Morning Intentions

Daily Affirmation:
_____
_____
_____

Today, I look forward to...
_____
_____
_____

What would make today amazing?
_____
_____
_____

Evening Reflections

What would make today greater?
_____
_____
_____

Best Moment of My Day:
_____
_____
_____

People I am grateful for...
_____
_____

REMEMBER:

Tomorrow I am looking forward to...
_____
_____

Journal Prompt

FREE YOURSELF !

Inspirational Quote:

Date:___/___/___
S / M / T / W / T / F / S

Morning Intentions

Daily Affirmation:

Today, I look forward to...

What would make today amazing?

Evening Reflections

What would make today greater?

Best Moment of My Day:

People I am grateful for...

REMEMBER:

Tomorrow I am looking forward to...

Journal Prompt

FREE YOURSELF !

Date:___/___/___
S / M / T / W / T / F / S

Inspirational Quote:

___

Morning Intentions

Daily Affirmation:

___

Today, I look forward to...

___

What would make today amazing?

___

Evening Reflections

What would make today greater?

___

Best Moment of My Day:

___

People I am grateful for...

REMEMBER:

Tomorrow I am looking forward to...

Journal Prompt

FREE YOURSELF !

Date:___/___/___
S / M / T / W / T / F / S

Inspirational Quote:

Morning Intentions

Daily Affirmation:

Today, I look forward to...

What would make today amazing?

Evening Reflections

What would make today greater?

Best Moment of My Day:

People I am grateful for...

REMEMBER:

Tomorrow I am looking forward to...

Journal Prompt

FREE YOURSELF !

Date:___/___/___
Inspirational Quote:
S / M / T / W / T / F / S

Morning Intentions

Daily Affirmation:

Today, I look forward to...

What would make today amazing?

Evening Reflections

What would make today greater?

Best Moment of My Day:

People I am grateful for...

REMEMBER:

Tomorrow I am looking forward to...

Journal Prompt

FREE YOURSELF !

Inspirational Quote:

Date:___/___/___
S / M / T / W / T / F / S

Morning Intentions

Daily Affirmation:

Today, I look forward to...

What would make today amazing?

Evening Reflections

What would make today greater?

Best Moment of My Day:

People I am grateful for...

REMEMBER:

Tomorrow I am looking forward to...

Journal Prompt

FREE YOURSELF !

Inspirational Quote:

Date:___/___/___
S / M / T / W / T / F / S

Morning Intentions

Daily Affirmation:

Today, I look forward to...

What would make today amazing?

Evening Reflections

What would make today greater?

Best Moment of My Day:

People I am grateful for...

REMEMBER:

Tomorrow I am looking forward to...

Journal Prompt

FREE YOURSELF !

Inspirational Quote:

Date:___/___/___
S / M / T / W / T / F / S

Morning Intentions

Daily Affirmation:

Today, I look forward to...

What would make today amazing?

Evening Reflections

What would make today greater?

Best Moment of My Day:

People I am grateful for...

REMEMBER:

Tomorrow I am looking forward to...

Journal Prompt

FREE YOURSELF !

Inspirational Quote:

Date:___/___/___
S / M / T / W / T / F / S

Morning Intentions

Daily Affirmation:

Today, I look forward to...

What would make today amazing?

Evening Reflections

What would make today greater?

Best Moment of My Day:

People I am grateful for...

REMEMBER:

Tomorrow I am looking forward to...

Journal Prompt
FREE YOURSELF !

Inspirational Quote:

Date:___/___/___
S / M / T / W / T / F / S

Morning Intentions

Daily Affirmation:

Today, I look forward to...

What would make today amazing?

Evening Reflections

What would make today greater?

Best Moment of My Day:

People I am grateful for...

REMEMBER:

Tomorrow I am looking forward to...

Journal Prompt

FREE YOURSELF !

Inspirational Quote:

Date:___/___/___
S / M / T / W / T / F / S

Morning Intentions

Daily Affirmation:

Today, I look forward to...

What would make today amazing?

Evening Reflections

What would make today greater?

Best Moment of My Day:

People I am grateful for...

REMEMBER:

Tomorrow I am looking forward to...

Journal Prompt

FREE YOURSELF !

Made in the USA
Monee, IL
17 January 2023